101

EDUCATIONAL

VITO PERRONE

Teaching Curriculum, and
Learning Environments Chair
at HARVARD UNIVERSITY

CHELSEA HOUSE PUBLISHERS
New York • Philadelphia

CONVERSATIONS

With Your
4th Grader

First Printing

1 3 5 7 9 8 6 4 2

Library of Congress Cataloging-in-Publication Data

Perrone, Vito.
  101 educational conversations to have with your child / Vito Perrone
p. cm. — (101 educational conversations to have with your child)
  Includes bibliographical references (p.) and index.
  ISBN 0-7910-1920-9
      0-7910-1985-3 (pbk.)
  1. Education—United States—Parent participation. 2. Fourth grade (Education)—
United States. 3. Parent and child—United States. 4. Communication—United
States. I. Title. II. Title: One hundred one educational conversations to have with
your fourth grader. III. Title: One hundred and one educational conversations to
have with your fourth grader. IV. Series: Perrone, Vito. 101 educational conversations to have with your child.
LB1048.5.P475 1993   92-36834
649'.68'0973—dc20   CIP

Cover photo: Addie Passen

CONTENTS

Unlike most countries, the United States does not have a formal national curriculum. In theory, each of the 15,000 school districts in the United States creates—with direction from state education agencies—its own curriculum. In practice, however, there are more similarities than differences among these curricula. What amounts to a national curriculum has been created through years of curriculum development by various national organizations related to the various subject areas, through the widespread use of textbooks prepared for a national market, and through standardized testing programs that are national in scope and are designed so that the performance of children in any grade can be compared to the performance of children in the same grade but in a different community or state.

As a result of these standardizing forces, children in North Dakota study much the same subjects in their social studies classes, for example, as students in Massachusetts and Washington. They study their neighborhoods in grades 1 and 2, their cities in grade 3, their states in grade 4, American history in grade 5, some form of world history in grade 6, Latin America and Canada in grade 7, American history in grade 8, civics or world history in grade 9, global history or American history in grade 10, American history in grade 11, and either American government and economics or an elective course in American history or world history in grade 12.

The science curriculum becomes somewhat standardized in grade 9 with the study of physical science or earth science. High school students study biology in grade 10, chemistry in grade 11, and either physics or an elective course in biology or physical science in grade 12. In mathematics they study algebra I in grade 9, geometry in grade 10, algebra II in grade 11, and either trigonometry and precalculus or calculus in grade 12.

Each volume in the *101 Educational Conversations You Should Have with Your Child* series contains an outline of the typical curriculum for that particular grade. But you will probably find it helpful to ask your child's teacher about the curriculum for each new grade your child enters. The teacher can give you a fuller account of what is being taught in your school system.

You and Your Child's Education

Welcome to *101 Educational Conversations with Your Fourth Grader,* one of a series of books for parents who wish to be more involved in their children's education. I have written these books with two important goals in mind—first, to give parents a solid basis for talking with their children about their school experiences and thereby gaining further insight into their children's growth as learners; and second, to guide parents toward constructive, education-oriented interaction with teachers and administrators in their children's schools.

In my 30 years of experience in and around schools, I have found that parents are not always clear about what their children are learning in school, about whether their children's overall education is powerful or trivial, challenging or dull. Furthermore, parents often lack a vision of what the schools—at their best—should provide students. We must acknowledge, of course, that not all of what children must ultimately know and understand is learned in the schools. However, the schools do have an intentional curriculum, regardless of the grade level.

In the elementary years, schools expect to teach children reading and writing, as well as certain aspects of science, social studies, and mathematics. They also expect to introduce children to the arts. These efforts should enable children not only to build upon what they learn at home but also to extend their classroom learning into the world outside school. Parents are a vital part of this endeavor. The more you know about the school's intentions and your child's responses, the better for your child's overall education.

Parents invariably ask their children, "What did you learn (or do) at school today?" and are treated to what has become the classic, predictable response: "Nothing." This is clearly a discouraging exchange, leaving parents on the outside or making them feel that they must press their children for details. But a parent's insistence only makes the exchange rather unnatural or even negative, with problematic results. Not only does the parent gain few new insights into the child's education, but the child may come to resent what he or she perceives as a grilling or as a routine, meaningless inquiry. The *101 Educational Conversations You Should Have with Your Child* series is designed to help parents get closer to what their children are learning. It encourages parents to find out what their children understand and also what they do not yet understand. The goal is to make parents' exchanges with their children about school and learning more natural and enjoyable, a mutual treat rather than a mutual burden.

At various times in the school year, parents are invited to parent-teacher conferences, where they often hear a good deal about their children's progress in different subjects. In most cases, however, parents bring too little to these meetings. Rather than being genuine conversations, the conferences are one-sided reports. Parents may leave these sessions satisfied enough, though in my experience few of them say that they are fully engaged by the process. The *101 Educational Conversations You Should Have with Your Child* series should contribute to constructive change. These books are intended to help you inform yourself about what the schools hope to teach and what your children are learning. You should then be able to bring to the parent-teacher conferences some of your own insights and perspectives about your children's educational growth. You will also be able to pose more potent questions to your children's teachers. As a result, your interactions with teachers should become more interesting and more constructive. The children and the schools will surely benefit.

An important premise of this series is that parents are their children's *first* teachers and their most critically important partners in learning. While this may seem most obvious to parents when their children are in the early primary grades, it is vital for parents to remain involved throughout their children's school lives. This is not, I grant, always easy. For one thing, parents often do not really know what the schools are teaching. In this regard the schools should be expected to provide much better information. Weekly guides would not be too much to expect. Nor would occasional workshops to give parents a fuller understanding of the questions children are asked in school, the books children read, and the principal objectives of the curriculum. If the schools do not deliver this kind of information to parents, then parents should ask, Why not?

Further, while schools typically say they value parent participation, parents are not always treated as full partners. This must change. If the schools do not actively acknowledge and encourage a strong role for parents, then parents themselves should take the initiative. Although this book is most concerned with the parent-child exchange, it will not have succeeded if it does not also empower parents in their relationships with their children's schools and teachers. In the end, the educational partnerships that we so desperately need—between parents and their children and between parents and schools—will be stronger.

101 Educational Conversations with Your Fourth Grader focuses on three areas of interest to parents:

- An overview of the fourth grade, with a look at how classrooms are organized, the kinds of experiences that are offered to children in school, and the basic curriculum—the content of what is taught.

- A collection of conversation starters and suggested activities— a how-to guide for parents who want to explore and expand their children's learning process through creative, stress-free interactions.

- A parent's guide to interacting with teachers and school administrators.

I wish to make one last point in this introduction. In the course of a school year, children study across many fields of inquiry. They read numerous books, view large numbers of films and videos, respond to many hundreds of questions, hear about a myriad of individuals and groups, explore the geography and politics of many countries, and learn many small facts and some larger conceptions. This book, and the others in this series, cannot cover *all* the ground that a child covers in a year. The most it can offer is a variety of useful places to begin. I expect that, once given these important guideposts, parents will be able to develop their own conversations and activities to enhance their understanding of their children's education while in turn enlarging the educational possibilities for the children. I trust that all of you who read this and the other books in the *101 Educational Conversations You Should Have with Your Child* series will have as good a time using the ideas as I and my colleagues have had in putting them together.

1 Your Child's Classroom

The best fourth grade classrooms are *developmentally appropriate*, as are *all* good elementary school classrooms. This means that most activities are based on the physical, intellectual, social, and emotional development of each child, *not* on the children's ages or grade levels. Most fourth grade children, for example, are very independent readers; others are still consolidating their mastery of reading. Some have mastered the computer keyboard; others are still tentative. Some are quite accomplished musicians; others are just beginning to feel comfortable with an instrument. Expecting all children to be at the same point, and teaching as if they were, not only limits the learning experience for many children but for some children induces feelings of failure that will not easily be overcome. Attention to individual development rather than emphasis on grade levels is very important. Teachers and schools must, of course, set standards of accomplishment, but they should not expect all children to reach these standards at the same time.

Developmentally appropriate classrooms are characterized by certain features. Among the most important of these are:

Respect for the Children

- Children's interests are important starting points for learning.

- Children's ideas and work are taken seriously.

- Children are understood to be actively in search of knowledge. Their questions, constructions, and observations are seen as part of the process of building knowledge.

- Children do as much talking as the teachers.

- Children have many opportunities to choose—the literature they read, the projects they do, the activities they participate in.

- Children have *time* to look around, wonder, and dream.

- Children work cooperatively, helping each other.

- Individual, racial, linguistic, and cultural differences are celebrated. They are seen as ways of enriching the children's lives.

Stimulation of Thought, Imagination, and Self-esteem

- As children move beyond information to understanding, teachers respond to children's ideas and questions in ways that extend their learning rather than with rote answers.

- Teachers (and children) ask more open-ended questions than yes-or-no questions. Teachers spark exchanges by saying, "What if we did it this way?" "How else could we do it?" "Who has thought of another way?" "Is there another viewpoint?" "Why was it like that?" ""How could it have been different?"

■ Considerable attention is given to the processes of exploration and discovery, inquiry and investigation.

■ Errors are generally seen as steps toward further learning, as particular inventions—not as mistakes or failures. Teachers respond to errors in ways that keep children's self-esteem intact and leave them eager to learn, not fearful of making mistakes.

■ Teachers encourage risk taking and provide a safe, supportive environment for it.

An Abundance of Chances To Learn

■ All forms of communication are given attention: reading, writing, listening, speaking. The classroom is full of language.

■ The classroom is inviting and colorful, with a variety of interesting materials. The children know where these materials are kept and how to use them.

■ Fourth grade children's learning activities rely more upon texts than was the case in the earlier grades. Yet real experiences, concrete materials, and hands-on activities are still important. Teachers help the children make connections between the various areas of study. To the greatest possible degree, knowledge is presented as an interconnected web, not as a handful of distinct categories that are unrelated to each other.

■ Teachers keep learning, and they share what they learn with their students. They demonstrate that learning is a lifelong process and a source of delight.

■ Children write their own books, which in turn can be read by others in the class; these writings increasingly reflect children's growing interest in the various subject matter fields, such as geography and science.

- Notes, letters, poems, song lyrics, and all forms of written information and expression are highly visible in the classroom.

- Children read real books by real authors, not just committee-produced "readers."

- Teachers know that learning takes place over time, and that children need numerous and related experiences before they are able to absorb critical concepts and use these concepts effectively as the basis of new learning.

- Interest in literature and social studies grows, matching the earlier interest in science and mathematics.

Opportunities for Self-expression and Connections to the Children's Life Outside School

- Children have frequent opportunities to participate in the creative and expressive arts: music, drawing, storytelling, drama.

- Children have frequent opportunities to run, climb, and play organized games. Physical activities are seen as important for health as well as for building self-confidence.

- Parents are welcome in the classroom. They are encouraged to be active participants in their children's education.

- Teachers make an effort to connect children's lives in school to experiences outside of school such as reading at home, getting a pet, taking a family vacation, eating a new food for the first time, seeing a movie with their parents, music lessons, organized sports activities, and the like.

Teachers who think in developmental terms understand that they can return often to a particular topic of study. Each time they do so, the children's levels of comprehension will have changed. A child who wants to learn more about West African traditions, for example, will not be told, "You learned about that last year" or "You'll learn about that when you get to the fifth grade." As much as possible, teachers should allow their presentation of material to be guided by the children's interests, acknowledging that inquiries from students are an important stimulus for learning.

In developmental classrooms, teachers often build the curriculum around themes. For instance, the children may be studying Plains Indians, such as the Sioux, Blackfoot, Crow, Mandan, Arikara, and Hidatsa. They will read about these people's strong ties to nature and the role of the buffalo in their way of life, and they will also read traditional Native American folktales. They will watch a video documentary or perhaps a movie about Indians. They will write animal stories in the style of one of the tribes, draw and paint designs used by the Plains Indians, and learn about and perform traditional dances. They may even learn some expressions in Plains sign language. Such units of study provide integration across nearly all of the subject areas.

Classroom Organization

Classrooms for the fourth through sixth grades have a different look from kindergarten through third grade classrooms. To some extent this reflects structural changes. In many schools, fourth grade students begin to do some of their work with people who are called specialist teachers. Children may spend two or three hours each day with one teacher who works mostly with language arts and social studies, and then they may go to other classrooms for instruction in math, science, physical education, foreign language, and the arts. In such arrangements, children usually study math and science daily (though not always for the same amount of time) and the arts and physical education twice a week.

The specialist teacher arrangement works best when all the teachers involved are members of a team that works consistently with the same children. When this is the case, the teachers can jointly plan the children's work around common themes. The work going on in social studies and literature, for example, can be related to what is being studied in math, science, and music. Moreover, all of the teachers will get to know the children well and can share insights about each child's strengths, questions, and possible problems. Such a team of teachers can provide focused support for each child.

You should know, however, that most schools that use specialist teachers *do not* use *teams* of teachers in this way. Instead, in far too many instances each teacher functions in an isolated matter, concentrating only on his or her particular subject, and the children may be exposed to a number of teachers, with little or no consistency over the course of a school year. Such arrangements promote few, if any, interrelationships among the various subjects. As a result, children's exposure to each subject is less intense; the deep understandings that schools should be promoting do not emerge as they should.

In other schools, however, children in the fourth through sixth grades continue to be taught in self-contained classrooms, with one teacher all day, every day. In most cases this is more effective than having children work with four or five teachers each day in a curriculum that is not well integrated.

However the classroom is organized, it should support a diversity of uses and contain a wide range of materials. The best classrooms will contain movable tables and chairs that can easily be arranged and rearranged. A box or cubby will be available to store each child's personal belongings; these spaces are treated with great respect by the teachers and the children.

While teachers will organize their classrooms according to their own preferences, the arrangements described below are not uncommon in fourth through sixth grade classrooms.

Print Materials and Equipment

Many books and magazines related to the various subject fields are freely available to the children. Reading materials will change frequently to accommodate the special topics being studied. (The classroom's collection of reading material includes books, reports, poems, and narratives written by the children; keeping alive a strong sense of authorship is important in the intermediate years.) Beyond the classroom collection, the children are encouraged to make frequent use of the school's main library as well as the local public library, for special research work and for access to a larger array of biographies and interesting fiction.

Equipment related to the entire spectrum of communications and problem solving is present: computers and at least one printer, a video monitor and tapes, audiotape recorders, drawing boards, and a considerable amount of scientific equipment—microscopes, magnets, pulleys, scales, motors. Children will also have access to easels and paints, a potter's wheel and clay, and musical instruments.

From the fourth grade on, children typically use textbooks in all the subject areas they are studying. These texts try to be comprehensive, which generally means that they cover a great deal of material—probably too much. And they are most often accompanied by numerous peripheral materials, including workbooks. But one major difficulty with these textbooks is that they appear to be so comprehensive that they often become virtually the sole basis for study in whatever subject area they cover: math, science, social studies, or literature. This inhibits teachers from guiding children toward a diversity of study materials and prevents children from forming an eclectic, more inclusive approach to learning. When reading and subject matter study are confined to textbooks, content is often covered too quickly and too superficially.

Standardized textbooks encourage a passive orientation to learning that should be resisted by teachers and parents, who should insist to their school boards that textbooks, if used, be regarded as one among many resources, not as the sole resources. Moreover, textbooks are generally written in a bland and colorless style that does little to make a child get excited about reading.

All classrooms—whether self-contained rooms where the children study all subject areas, or rooms designed to serve as study sites for a particular subject area—should be rich environments with a wide range of learning materials. The teachers will consider it important that the children know what materials are available, where they are stored, and how to use them. By this point in their school lives, the children have learned how to use the tools and equipment safely, and they have virtually complete access to all materials. Teachers know that if children do not know what is available to them, or if they must ask permission to use the items (which usually involves waiting), they may lose interest, and their opportunities for exploration will be limited. It should be noted, too, that children in such classrooms do things for themselves: they mix paints and clean brushes, and they operate video systems, tape recorders, and computers. These simple tasks are part of the process of learning self-reliance and responsibility.

2 *What Parents Want To Know*

Parents of intermediate grade school children often ask how large or small the class should be. Parents have an intuitive sense that the class should be small during the earliest years of school, from kindergarten through third grade. But class size is also very important in the fourth through sixth grades. Ideally, a fourth grade classroom should have fewer than 22 children, although 22 to 25 is an acceptable size. Class size should be designed to allow plenty of individual attention. The more attention the teacher can give to each child, and the more experiences the teacher can help each child have, the better. As class size goes beyond 25 students, the potential for individual interaction decreases considerably.

In the previous chapter, I explained the importance of having an abundance of varied learning materials in the classroom. My experience is that as class size goes beyond 25 children—which is too often the norm—the classroom becomes a less rich environment for each child. Teachers and parents need to become much more vocal about the importance of class size in these intermediate years.

Another question that comes up often is, How much homework is reasonable for fourth grade children? Most teachers do not assign much formal homework during the early years, but *some* homework could be useful, especially if it is interesting, if it goes beyond the daily school activities, and if it is aimed at deepening the child's understanding of what is being studied. A good homework assignment, prompted by a powerful question, might ask the student to interpret, synthesize, or reconstruct something (an idea or problem).

Homework assignments in the fourth grade might include: Read the new story you wrote to your mother or father. Read for 30 minutes on your own. Think about words related to outer space, or mountains, or agriculture. Write a narrative about what it would be like to be a child in some earlier time—perhaps when Columbus sailed to America or when the Wright brothers flew the first airplane. Watch a particular program on television and note the number of instances of violence in it. Draw a picture of the moon and the stars closest to it. Study a political cartoon in today's newspaper and be ready to describe its meaning in school tomorrow; ask yourself, What is the artist trying to say? Is the cartoon fair? Do you agree with the artist's idea?

A fourth grader might also be expected to complete some mathematics problems or to collect specimens of water from various sources—household faucets, ponds, puddles, and rain, for example— for a science experiment. But fourth grade children should *not* have homework that takes more than 60 minutes. If their homework assignments regularly exceed this limit, parents should inquire about it. And if there is *no* homework, that too is worth an inquiry.

I am often asked about the use of computers. Many children today use computers at home at age five or six, and a growing number of schools have installed computers in primary grade classrooms. Much can be done with computers, especially in word processing, mathematics, and problem-solving exercises. And some of the programs now available give children access to large museums and artistic collections as well as to various archives and their documents. In addition, some video games—especially those, such as detective games, that emphasize problem solving—could be used in the classroom. By fourth grade, children should be far along in their ability to use the computer for a variety of purposes.

Parents of intermediate-age children often ask about foreign language study. Some schools—and the numbers are still very small—begin foreign languages in the early primary grades, often in two-way bilingual programs. In such programs, half the children might be Spanish speaking, for example, and the other half speak no Spanish. Each group learns the other's language.

In most schools that offer foreign language study for elementary students, however, such study usually begins in the intermediate grades. The United States is far behind most other industrialized countries in second-language programs. *All* schools should offer a second language at the intermediate level, if not before. Studying a second language not only provides valuable insights into another culture and enriches the child's world but also greatly strengthens the child's understanding of his or her native language. Parents can and should do more to make sure that their children's schools understand the importance of foreign language programs.

A Parent's Guide to Teachers' Terminology

As they become involved with their children's schools, parents will hear teachers use many special terms to describe what happens in the classroom. Some of the most important terms are explained below.

LEARNING STYLES

Children learn in many different ways, although each child has a preference for one or two particular ways of learning. These preferences are called *learning styles*. Some children learn most easily when ideas, concepts, and information are first presented visually, through pictures or videos. Others gain understanding only after firsthand work such as writing, experimenting, problem solving, or playacting. Some children need to have ideas presented in a very precise and sequential order; for others, close attention to sequence complicates learning rather than promoting it. Teachers are most effective when they know children well enough to understand their individual learning styles. This lets them individualize each child's learning experiences.

BASAL TEXTS

Basal texts are textbooks designed to provide all students with a common base of information and generally proceed from easier to more difficult ideas. They are available in all subjects and are generally accompanied by numerous prepackaged materials, including workbooks. In the primary grades basal texts are used mainly for reading and language arts, but in the intermediate years they begin to be used for all subject areas. Whatever the grade or subject, though, if basal texts are rigidly followed they do not match the principles of developmentally appropriate classrooms, and they limit what is learned.

The basal text assumes that all children of the same age start from the same point. This is especially the case with the language arts texts, but it is true as well of the textbooks in math, science, and social studies. Because everything in these programs is sequential, those who begin the program with less language experience, prior knowledge, or confidence tend to stay behind as readers. Children do not need this kind of negative experience with learning.

LITERATURE-BASED READING PROGRAMS

Literature-based reading programs, often called "whole language programs," take a different approach to reading and the language arts than do the basal texts. In a literature-based program, children read works by identified authors—books and stories such as Madeleine L'Engle's *Wrinkle in Time*, Charles Dickens's *Oliver Twist*, Washington Irving's "Rip Van Winkle," and Mark Twain's "The Celebrated Jumping-Frog of Calaveras County." A classroom using this approach to reading will contain many books, both fiction and nonfiction, on a variety of topics and at many levels of complexity. Some of these books will be relatively easy to read, others more difficult. The children make choices about which books they read. A growing number of teachers believe that literature-based reading programs are not only more appropriate developmentally than skill-based basal reading programs but help the children become more effective as readers and writers.

DISCOVERY LEARNING

In classrooms organized around discovery learning, children are encouraged to ask questions, investigate subjects that interest them, and find solutions to problems. Teachers tend not to provide answers but rather to help children seek their own answers. Teachers encourage questions by raising questions themselves, by filling the classrooms with interesting materials, and by drawing upon many of the children's own experiences.

Suppose, for example, a child wants to know more about the importance of rain forests. The teacher might ask the child what ideas he or she already has about finding the information and then suggest additional avenues for exploration. The conversation might go like this:

TEACHER: How could you find out more about rain forests?

CHILD: Read, look in the encyclopedia or a book about the environment, find rain forests on a map, call the science museum, ask my older sister.

TEACHER: If you used the map, what would you expect to learn?

CHILD: I guess . . . where the rain forests are.

TEACHER: Let's look at a map together and see what information it provides about rain forests.

Here is another example of the kind of exchange that is heard in discovery-based classrooms:

TEACHER: How would you know where to place our plants to make sure they get the most sunlight?

CHILD: Well, we could see where north is, and then we could put the plants near a window on the east side of the room.

TEACHER: How could we find out where north and east are? Why would we do that? Are there any other possibilities?

The teacher's role in the discovery-based classroom is to help children find many of their own solutions by giving them a framework for asking and answering questions. Essentially, the teacher introduces children to additional ways of thinking and solving problems.

COOPERATIVE LEARNING

Cooperative learning is a means of helping children work together in order to increase their learning. Cooperative learning groups are organized to allow students to work on projects together, solve mathematics and science problems, do experiments, share stories, read to each other, and the like. Groups of three or four children working together are particularly effective. In such groups the children will take turns being the moderator, the recorder/reporter, or the monitor of the group's progress.

BALANCE

Teachers throughout the elementary grades, especially those who lean toward developmentally appropriate teaching, talk a good deal about the need for balance. Balance means quiet times followed by active times followed by quiet times; times when children work alone and times when they work with others; times to explore and times to consolidate learning. The days must be varied and should address the needs of the "whole child."

ASSESSMENT

Assessment refers to determinations about children's progress. More and more educational professionals, at least those involved in elementary education, recommend that we stop relying on traditional standardized tests, which typically evaluate children on the basis of fixed standards of skill, achievement, or intelligence and often contribute to misjudgments about children's learning.

The current trend in the lower grades of elementary school is away from standardized testing. I do not recommend the use of standardized tests before grade 4, but even in the intermediate grades their benefits are uncertain, especially if they are used to make judgments about individual children. Instead of using externally developed, standardized tests, teachers can more appropriately assess students by keeping ongoing records of their performance, documenting students' work on a day-by-day basis. Teachers also keep portfolios of children's work; these are available for the children as well as their parents to review. You will find your child's actual performance in ongoing instructional activities far more informative than any standardized test. Teachers also guide children in systematic and regular self-evaluation. By asking, for example, "Do you feel that you understood what we talked about in science today? Do you think you could explain it to a friend? What do you think was most difficult?" teachers encourage children to define their own learning processes and help them set goals.

THE TEACHER AS FACILITATOR

A facilitator is someone who makes it easier for another to do something. Teachers who guide, question, and support children in their learning are facilitators; they make it easier for children to learn, but they give the central role in the learning process to the children themselves. Teachers who see themselves as facilitators stimulate children and challenge them to think and question. They provide a diversity of materials and activities, and they search for new books and questions that will extend children's learning and enlarge their awareness. They spend much of their time supporting children's investigations. In contrast, teachers who "give answers" most of the time and who do most of the talking in the classroom are not facilitators.

3 *Your Child's School Day*

What is your child's school day like? In the primary grades—at least through grade 3, and particularly in classrooms organized around the principles of developmental learning—the school day tends to be rather fluid. In these early grades there are few hard-and-fast demarcations between subject areas.

But in the intermediate grades the various subjects become more defined, and the day becomes somewhat more structured. The use of specialist teachers for some subjects adds further structure to the daily schedule in schools that follow this practice. In too many cases the daily schedule in grade 4 is rigidly fixed and compartmentalized—although it would be better if the school day retained more of the fluid, integrated character of the earlier grades.

THE MORNING
Typically the first half hour of the school day (from 8:30 to 9:00 A.M.) is devoted to opening activities: announcements, discussions of special events, the sharing of a poem that someone in the class enjoys or has recently written, possibly a song, and reminders about what needs to be accomplished during the day. This opening

session is a way of bringing everyone together; it both creates a transition from the previous day and also builds a strong feeling of community in the classroom.

On at least three days each week, language arts and social studies are the focus during the course of the morning (between 9:00 A.M. and noon). This might mean half an hour devoted to uninterrupted sustained silent reading, when everyone—including the teacher— reads, followed by an hour-long writing workshop in which the children work on fiction and nonfiction narratives, poems, and biographies. During the latter period the children will typically read their work aloud to others for response, rework what they have done, and have individual and small-group conferences with the teacher. The teacher will often do some minilessons during this time—for example, demonstrating the appropriate places to use an exclamation point, a semicolon, a colon; pointing out some new and interesting words being used by members of the class; or helping the children understand how and when to use different verb tenses.

Social studies is the focus during the 40 minutes or so before lunch. Much of the activity takes place in cooperative groups. Further, it will be reasonably well connected to the language arts activities. For example, the books that the children read during the morning's silent reading period and the stories or essays they write in the writing workshop are likely to involve a subject that will be discussed in social studies.

Two mornings a week the children focus on music, a foreign language, or physical education, for approximately 35 minutes each. Physical education in the fourth grade is generally concerned with movement and running. The children play a variety of ball games, and they may dance or do movement exercises. (If they have music and foreign language in the morning, they will have physical education sometime in the afternoon, and vice versa).

THE AFTERNOON

At least three afternoons each week, the period from 12:30 to 2:30 P.M. is devoted to mathematics and science. Often this instruction is provided by specialist teachers.

The children spend the final period of the day (2:30 to 3:15 P.M.) with their primary teacher, who is usually the person with whom they spent the morning. During this end-of-day session the teacher reads to the children, often from a classic book that is related to the diverse cultural traditions of the students. It might be Lorraine Hansberry's *Raisin in the Sun* or Diane Wolkstein's *Banza: A Haitian Story*. Such a book might take several weeks to complete; this extended reading provides a thread of continuity and reinforces the children's sustained concentration skills.

The late afternoon is also devoted to clarifying homework assignments and to journal writing. Students' entries in their journals might center around such questions as "What did I do today in math? In science? What did I learn that was important? What wasn't clear to me? What don't I understand?" Such self-evaluation at the completion of each school day is important. It teaches children to turn their growing analytical and reflective skills upon themselves, and it gives them a feeling of participation, ownership, and control over their own education that will become increasingly important as they advance through school.

4
What Your Child Learns in School

This chapter is an overview of the typical curriculum for the fourth grade. It is intended to give you an idea of what your child is learning in school. But because children learn in different ways and at different rates, not all children will grasp a particular part of the curriculum at the same time. While most fourth grade children will master the typical fourth grade curriculum outlined below, others will need more time to solidify their understanding of some subjects. Teachers and parents who understand development, who do not view the curriculum in terms of rigid grades or steps, will accept this as quite normal.

I have outlined fourth grade content, but keep in mind that some elements from the previous year's curriculum are carried into the fourth grade; such overlap is both common and helpful. And while I have divided the curriculum into different subject areas for convenience, in reality the boundaries between subject areas are not always so clearly drawn. In fact, the learning environment is better when the demarcations between subjects are not sharp and students are encouraged to focus on the connections, rather than the distinctions, in a body of knowledge. Unfortunately, subject matter delineations take hold in a big way in too many fourth grade classrooms. Social studies suddenly becomes separate from reading, math from science, and so on. It would benefit fourth grade children if this trend were reversed.

Parents should also be aware that while teaching in the first few grades is more informal than formal, formality and structure increase in and after the fourth grade. Even in the intermediate years, however, children's learning requires concreteness and active experiences. In the best fourth grade classrooms, children continue to learn through activities and concrete experiences as well as through the teacher imparting information and interputing ideas and concepts.

One last point needs to be made about the curriculum. I have refrained from listing all of the *specific* elements that make up the various curriculum areas: the math facts that are learned, the books that are read, the historical figures who are presented. Teachers must introduce children at every grade level to a diverse and rich array of literature and to the many people who make up the traditions of their communities and of the country; at the same time, they must involve children in the fullest use of mathematics, science, and the like. The curriculum should always be expansive, never limiting. A good curriculum is flexible, so that the teacher can easily add not only new subject matter but new levels of complexity. The teacher's main responsibility throughout elementary school is to ensure that children maintain a sense of curiosity, that they love reading and writing, and that they take an ongoing interest in the world around them. The teacher's job is to help children become and remain active and confident learners. That is more important than any particular set of facts.

In doing this job, teachers will probably use a good deal of traditional children's literature. But they may find that songs or stories from their children's cultural heritages have greater potential to stimulate children's language development and expand their learning. Similarly, the traditional heroes and narratives of United States history will surely emerge in the classroom. But knowing that the traditional histories often excluded women and persons of color, teachers will take care to expose the children to other, less traditional heroes and narratives. And by using math in many different ways and contexts, children gain control of the rules governing addition, subtraction, multiplication, and division. They also come to understand the patterns and relationships by which numbers are governed.

The curriculum throughout the intermediate grades should be rich and full of diverse starting points so that each child—with his or her individual interests, learning styles, and level of development—can enter fully into the learning process. The material being studied should never be so narrowly focused that there is no room for children to pursue some aspect of what interests them most. Suppose a class is studying the topic "the largest cities in our state," for example. Some children might want to examine the earliest histories of one or more cities, while others might want to give more attention to what the cities are like today. Some children might focus on changes in economic patterns—how products and industries in the region changed over time—while others might be more interested in the architecture of different periods. Some might want to learn more about how a city's neighborhoods developed; others might be curious about the city's cultural institutions or about famous people who lived there. The curriculum must be flexible enough to accommodate all these interests, and it must give the children opportunities to share their discoveries with one another. Above all, the curriculum must always be intellectually challenging.

As I noted in the introduction, teachers should be expected to have clear goals for the children they teach. They should be able to explain what the children will understand, or be able to do, by the end of the school year, and how everything they do in the classroom is related to those goals. Teachers should also be able to explain how they assess each child's progress toward those goals and how they will stay in touch with parents.

The Fourth Grade Curriculum

Most children entering the fourth grade are reasonably confident readers and writers. They are generally able to read a wide range of books, allowing the teacher to present them with an ever-growing diversity of reading and learning experiences. Moreover, fourth grade children are able to read for information as well as for enjoyment.

Fourth grade children will also understand the patterns of mathematical relationships and will be able to use math to solve basic computational problems; will know how to approach science questions and set up experiments; will be careful observers of the natural environment; will understand the importance of good health; will understand history as a human story; will appreciate the interdependency of people in their communities and across the nation and the world; will see themselves and their families as producers and consumers; will comprehend geographical relationships such as direction and geographical concepts such as place, elevation, latitude, and longitude; will enjoy the arts and recognize their place in society; and will see themselves as creators in various art forms. Most important, it is hoped that fourth grade children will continue to be curious about the world, will be confident that they can learn and will be filled with the desire to do so, and will be optimistic.

Beginning in the fourth grade, children experience a rapid widening of their horizons. They are aware of more of the world, and more is expected of them both at home and at school. During this time it is important that children's confidence be maintained—that they *not* come to say about the work in school, "It's too hard," or "I'm not good at math and science," or "I can't do it." Teachers may be principally responsible for motivating and supporting children at school, but parents must take special care to do the same thing at home.

LANGUAGE ARTS:
READING, WRITING, AND SPEAKING

As children enter the fourth grade, most are reasonably confident readers and writers, and they have also learned to use spoken language successfully. They are able to use books for enjoyment and as useful sources of information. They also know how to use a library and are comfortable doing so. They use writing for a variety of purposes; they understand the writing process, including the value of responses from their peers and revisions; and they have a good sense of authorship. They can also use spoken language effectively in a variety of settings—in discussions, oral reports, plays, explanations, and the like.

Where reading is concerned, the teacher's main task in grade four—and throughout the intermediate grades—is to *keep* children reading. This means continually enlarging classroom libraries, making extensive use of school and community libraries, referring the children to new books, talking about books, reading to the children from ever-more-complex works, and working with librarians and other teachers to organize such events as schoolwide book fairs and author visits for the children.

While some schools have organized the language arts curriculum around American literature in fourth and fifth grades, most teachers believe it is more important to keep children reading many different kinds of literature, as their interests guide them, than to concentrate on a particular country, genre, or period. Children need to know that when they become readers, a very large world is available to them. In the best settings, teachers will do everything they can to help children step into that large world—and stay in it.

Writing is closely related to reading. Teachers should make sure that children write every day and that they see themselves as active communicators: writers of journals and letters, authors of poetry, biography, and fiction. Teachers know that writing improves with practice, and that writing and thinking are closely intertwined, so they hold daily writing workshops—periods when children write, revise, and discuss their work. In some schools teachers say that there is not enough time for daily writing workshops. There has to be time!

By the fourth grade each child should have a well-established writing portfolio that contains files of his or her past writing, recently completed works, and writing in progress. Viewing this work over time is important to a child's self-evaluation and growth; in addition, the portfolio helps the teacher determine what kind of guidance and assistance each child needs. In the best schools, portfolios are maintained through the intermediate grades.

Fourth grade children will be writing cursive script rather than printing. They should get a good deal of practice with cursive writing in the course of their studies, although they will also do much of their formal writing—reports, essays, and the like—on the computer. Because teachers know that autobiographical and reflective writing is a good means of reinforcing the writing-thinking connection, children are encouraged to keep journals in which they record questions and insights about the various subjects they study as well as personal reflections.

Children will have many chances to practice most writing conventions, including punctuation marks, paragraphing, and verb tenses. They will also learn to write dialogues, explanations, and comparisons, although their skills in these areas will be at the beginner's level.

The oral aspects of language—especially effective speaking—are always important. Teachers view both speaking and listening as closely related to reading and writing. Children are given many opportunities to speak in a variety of contexts: telling and retelling stories, participating in focused discussions about particular topics, sharing information with other children, giving formal speeches, appearing in plays and readers' theater, reading published poems or their own writings aloud. They are also encouraged to examine how language is used in the home, the neighborhood, and the media and to develop an understanding of the power of the spoken word.

MATHEMATICS

In the fourth grade, mathematics continues to be something that is *used,* something children see as extending far beyond school. While children are expected to do basic computational functions such as adding, substracting, dividing, and multiplying, in the best classrooms math consists of much more than worksheets filled with problems or drills on number facts. Children learn *when* to add and subtract, to use a calculator, to estimate, and to arrange information on a graph. They begin to have an understanding of probability and how to judge it. They are encouraged to see how relationships among numbers, patterns, or events can be made more understandable with mathematical formulations, and they establish models for problem solving.

Teachers spend a good deal of time helping the children develop mental models—that is, teaching the children how to visualize problems and solutions. They will also ask the children to develop personal theories by thinking about different ways to solve mathematical problems. Because math cannot be completely understood at this age, when it stands apart from all other subjects, math will continue to be used in social studies, science, and language arts work.

You should expect to see your fourth grade child become a much better estimator than he or she was before. Further, your child will be able to see patterns in numbers more easily—they will note in a sequence of 1, 2, 4, 8 that subsequent numbers will be 16, 32, 64—and will have some beginning understanding of probabilities: how likely is it that when flipping a coin, heads will come out 2 times more than tails, etc. The child should also be able to measure things with precision and to manage fractions fairly well—although, because of their use of calculators, children are increasingly familiar with decimals. Teachers often ask the children, "How can we solve this problem?" For example, the teacher might present the following problem: "If 10 balls cost $46.25, how much would 26 balls cost?" The emphasis would be less on finding the correct answer than on showing that there are multiple ways of approaching the problem.

The goal of mathematics in the fourth grade is to help children maintain a good sense of what numbers mean and to make them feel that math is as commonplace and accessible as any other subject in school. Mathematics is *not* a mystery that only a select few can master. It should be—and in the best settings it is—fully available to all.

SCIENCE AND HEALTH

Children's interest in science often seems to decline in grade four and after. I suspect that this happens because science study is too often textbook-driven, passive, formal, and narrow in its scope. But the major goal of science study in these grades should be to keep children interested in science and cause them to believe that they can be successful science students. Not an easy task—but one that is critically important.

It is vital that children see and recognize "science" all around them in their everyday lives. Basic scientific principles are at work whenever a child rides a bicycle, puts air in the bike's tires and oils the moving parts, runs, throws a ball, gets water from a well or a faucet, uses a flashlight, takes pictures with a camera, or flies a kite. And science is also a basis for understanding what is happening when a child watches cloud formations change or planes move across the sky, plants a garden or trims bushes, reads about drought and gypsy moth infestations, or sees the effects of aging or infirmity in others. Good teachers draw heavily on such examples of "science in the world."

The natural world was the focus of science study during the primary years of school. While nature studies continue during the intermediate years, technology comes in for an increasing share of attention in the fourth grade and thereafter. Children learn about and examine machines of all kinds, including computers and mass communication systems. They are often asked about the role of technology "in our lives."

Meteorology is also studied in many fourth grade classrooms. Children gain a fairly sophisticated understanding of weather patterns, wind directions, temperature, precipitation, air pressure with high and low systems, and so on. Children will examine weather maps and follow weather reports on television.

The intermediate years are a good time for classes to visit science museums, or for scientists and technologists to visit classrooms. Children may be exposed to more of these experiences in the fourth grade than in earlier grades.

Inquiry—an open-ended approach to the study of science—also assumes a larger role once students enter the fourth grade. Children will be asked to engage in the process of inquiry, experimenting with ways of finding answers both to their own questions and to questions posed by the teacher. Such questions might include: What shapes or designs will support the most weight? Why do some objects stand and others fall? How much of the school's waste is recyclable? Where in your home is the humidity greatest, and why? What are the effects, if any, of light and darkness on fish? What causes things to either float or sink in water, or in vinegar, or in water mixed with oil? Children's questions are unending, and good teachers use those questions to teach the children about the process of inquiry—how to go about examining something. The children thus do what scientists do: define a problem and then figure out how to solve it.

In regard to the study of health, children continue the exploration of the life cycle that was begun in the earlier grades. What it means to stay healthy—to maintain wellness—cannot be overemphasized. Fourth grade children will pay attention to life-styles. They examine life-style choices such as smoking, and they learn about the effects of various kinds of consumption upon health, as well as upon the environment. They also learn something about medicine and its effect on health. And because fourth graders are moving rapidly toward puberty, some attention is given to bodily changes and the further changes that children can expect as they grow.

SOCIAL STUDIES

History and geography begin to become distinct fields of study in the fourth grade, although they should be linked whenever possible to what is being studied in language arts and in science. By fourth grade children know how to use several different kinds of maps. Further, they are able to use primary sources—historical records, diaries, newspapers, and the like—to enlarge their understanding of other people and other time periods; and they have had some experience interviewing their parents and grandparents about other times. These skills are enhanced during the intermediate grades as children continue to work with maps and primary documents, and make use of active inquiry around questions they pose.

At the same time, children are helped to frame historical questions in a more conceptual fashion: Why did that happen? What other possibilities were there? What were the effects? How do we know? How have things changed or stayed the same since then?

The fourth grade curriculum concentrates on state history and geography, although American history is necessarily part of these studies. But in the best classrooms, the social studies curriculum also continues to follow world events. Furthermore, the teacher uses the children's interests as the springboard for investigations into people's origins in Europe, Africa, Asia, or Latin America. Social studies also expands children's knowledge and appreciation of the literature of legends, those mythical stories that have been handed down across the generations. Children in the intermediate and middle school years tend to be attracted to the mythic, and mythic stories can teach much about various peoples and cultures. Traditional stories about King Arthur, Merlin the magician, and the Round Table are just the beginning. Children can also read legends about Atlantis, El Dorado, Romulus and Remus, Zoroaster, Yahuar Huacac, and the Native American mythic and folk heroes.

Regarding state history, children generally study such subjects as the geographic environment over time; glaciers and their effect on land forms (where appropriate); the Native American inhabitants and their ways of life; the European entry; and the development of towns, cities, and governmental structures. Children will read biographies of people who lived in their state or influenced its history. Children will also make more visits to historical sites and museums, and they will make a variety of personal investigations that might involve interviewing family and community members about past events, visiting a county courthouse to see old records, and the like. Finally, teachers will encourage the children to read the daily newspaper, watch news on television, and talk regularly with their parents or guardians about local, state, national, and world events.

THE ARTS

Experience with the arts is important throughout elementary school. Children often have specialist art teachers, especially in the intermediate grades. These twice-weekly sessions are most often devoted to vocal music, which is certainly beneficial; yet it would be far better if the arts program also included regular sessions of dance, painting, and instrumental music. The arts have an unstable history in our schools—arts programs are sometimes viewed as less important than other programs, and they are often among the first to be cut when budgets are tight. Parents should therefore be vigilant, insisting that strong, balanced arts programs are essential and must be made available to their children.

Ideally, the classroom time devoted to the arts program is supplemented by after-school enrichment programs and small group lessons, particularly in music and the visual arts. The intermediate years are an especially fertile time for children who are interested in string instruments. Many children develop new interests in music at this time, and their physical growth enables them to handle a bow, to manipulate strings, and to hear sounds better than they could before.

Fourth grade children, like younger children, are readily drawn to painting as a means of self-expression, and they are also attracted to group choral singing. The fourth grade is a good time to make art museums, art exhibitions, and musical performances a regular part of the curriculum. Teachers and parents can also encourage children to watch performance programs on public television; these broadcasts can do a great deal to enrich children's knowledge and appreciation of a wide range of music and drama. Even opera can be quite accessible and enjoyable to a child, if care is taken to tell the child what to expect and how to interpret what he or she views.

One way fourth grade teachers integrate the arts into the curriculum is by having the children read biographies of musicians, dancers, and painters as part of their language arts work; children can also read the lyrics of both classical and contemporary songs. Another way children gain enhanced awareness of the arts is by putting on plays or concerts for which they design and paint sets and write scripts and music. In social studies, the arts are introduced as cultural aspects of life—for example, various art forms can be related to their regions of origin. Even science touches the arts when topics such as sound and color appear in the science curriculum.

5

Conversations with Your Child

This chapter presents an array of "conversation starters" for you to use with your fourth grade child. I use the term *conversation* broadly, to include both question-and-answer dialogues and a variety of games and activities. The conversation starters are grouped by subject matter: the language arts and the creative arts, math, science and health, and social studies. Most of the ideas and suggestions I offer are broad and open-ended; some, however, are quite specific. And many of the conversation starters can be adapted and expanded by imaginative parents (and children) for an almost infinite number of possibilities.

Some of the conversations that are introduced in this volume of the *101 Educational Conversations You Should Have with Your Child* series appeared in the earlier volume, *101 Educational Conversations with Your Third Grader.* Most of these, however, have been reframed to accommodate the greater maturity and knowledge of the fourth grader. Such overlapping will also occur in later volumes of the series. In part this overlapping occurs because the curriculum is often interconnected from year to year. But the overlap also reflects the developmental character of learning—the same ideas are right for different children at different ages. And returning to the same conversations or activities a year or more from now will let you see how your child's knowledge and understanding have grown.

During the intermediate grades, factual information begins to take on ever greater importance in your child's education. Each year's curriculum reflects the growing importance of a knowledge base, and so, therefore, do the conversations I offer as your child progresses through school. The learning process itself—and the mental and emotional qualities that promote effective learning—continue to be of paramount importance, but your educational conversations with your child will inevitably involve more and more information and deeper understandings. Do not let this prospect alarm you—it is *not* necessary that you always know more than your child, or that you know the answer to every question your child asks. Indeed, you should expect your child to know more than you about a variety of subjects that he or she is studying in school. You can learn a lot from your children and about their education simply by asking them to share their growing knowledge base with you. By encouraging your child with comments such as "I don't understand that—could you explain it to me?" you can do much to strengthen his or her understanding of the subject in question, and perhaps your own understanding as well.

Do not be discouraged if some of the conversations and activities in this and later books appear to require knowledge that you do not have at your fingertips. It is not always necessary for you to know the answer to a question that you pose to your child; in fact, sometimes it is both more fun and more helpful to the child for the two of you to look up the answer together. You may want to familiarize yourself with some basic reference tools, either at home or at your library: a dictionary, an encyclopedia, and an atlas would be good places to start. You can also read through your child's school-books. The schools could contribute to this process as well—fourth grade might be a good time for the schools to begin presenting occasional parents' workshops, at which parents can get "refresher courses" in the material their children are studying.

The conversation starters that follow are a way for you to discover what your child knows and understands in relation to what is typically taught in the schools. You should remember, however, that the curriculum is not identical in every school; a gap in your child's learning may simply mean that that particular subject has not yet been introduced in the classroom. Be satisfied if your child can engage in *most* of these conversations, even with partial knowledge or limited understanding. You can always return to problem areas later on, as your child's mastery increases. But what about areas of learning that appear to be entirely outside a child's knowledge? A fourth grade child, for example, may appear to know very little about poetry, either how to read it or how to write it. While poetry is part of the curriculum in most schools, I do not believe that this particular gap in knowledge is necessarily a serious problem; parents themselves can help children with this kind of learning by reading and writing poetry together. But the parents might, nonetheless, ask the child's teacher, "What are you doing to help the children read and write poetry?" On the other hand, if a fourth grade child shows little interest in any kind of writing or is struggling to make sense of a map, the parents should certainly talk with the teacher, even as they spend more time writing with their child and looking at maps together.

The following ideas have been framed as conversational exchanges or playful interactions, not as daily quizzes. They are designed to promote interaction between parents and children. And because conversation does not flourish when questions lend themselves to simple answers—"yes," "no," and "I don't know"—most of the questions and activities have an open-ended quality. Try not to make them seem like tests or like some form of Trivial Pursuit. Instead, work them naturally into the time you spend with your child. The conversations should occur in a relaxed, comfortable context—at dinner, during a walk or a game, perhaps in relation to shared television programs or movies, or at some quiet time.

In a fundamental way, these conversations are educational opportunities. They allow you not only to reinforce what your child's teacher is doing but to expand the teacher's efforts, enriching your child's education. I believe that parents will, in the process of engaging in the conversations, realize more fully that they too are important and capable teachers. An additional benefit is that parents who take part in these exchanges will show their children that learning is a valuable activity, one that is capable of providing pleasure and worthy of respect.

The conversations are built around some important assumptions. I have assumed that parents

- Read to their children frequently.
- Listen to their children, respond to their questions, and engage them in ongoing conversations.
- Find opportunities to play with their children—physically active games as well as board games.
- Take walks with their children—around the block, through the parks, to a local playground.
- Take their children to the library, zoos, museums, and nature trails.
- Listen to records and tapes with their children.

- Let their children help them cook, wash the car, or rake leaves.
- Watch television with their children and discuss the content of programs with them.
- Share family stories with their children.

By enjoying their children regularly and naturally in the course of these and other activities, parents come to know a great deal about their children's growth as learners. The questions, activities, and ideas in this chapter will tell parents even more about their children—particularly about what their children are learning in school.

As you go through these conversations, keep in mind that fourth grade children are being exposed to a great deal of information in school and are still in the process of consolidating many ideas and relationships. Moreover, they are trying to make sense of what they are learning, striving for deeper understanding and for mastery of skills. If, for example, children learn various science facts but cannot use them for purposes they actually understand, cannot make connections between the facts and the world they see around them, then science is not becoming a particularly important subject matter. For science and for all subject areas, true understanding is far more important than a jumble of factual information that has little use beyond school and does not lead to more accelerated learning.

All-Purpose Conversation Starters

Many conversations between you and your child can arise spontaneously from day-to-day events. You can create numerous opportunities for such interactions in the following ways:

- Look at all the materials your child brings home from school. You will see a variety of things, including work sheets, word lists, books, classification exercises, writing samples, sculptures, paintings, and sketches. Ask your child about them. Say, "This looks interesting. Can you tell me how you did it?" or "I see you are learning about the ways electricity is generated. Are you doing any experiments with electricity? What have you learned?" Remember to be supportive rather than judgmental. If your child does not regularly bring writing, books, drawings, constructions, experiments, or paintings home from school, you should be concerned.

- Take note of your child's games and conversations with other family members and with friends. By looking closely at what your child brings home from school and how your child acts out new knowledge or skills while playing, you can keep in touch with elements of your child's education. These observations form a significant part of what you know about your child.

Certain questions that promote conversation between you and your child are versatile enough to apply in just about any situation. They may already be part of your repertoire. If not, start working them into your conversations. Use them often, but always—to repeat a point I made earlier in this chapter—use them patiently and naturally.

The questions are: "I wonder why that is?" "What do you think is happening?" "Is there any other way to do it?" "What if you tried it that way?" These questions and the many variations you can invent not only help keep dialogue going but also stimulate inquiry and discovery.

Language and the Arts

Throughout the elementary years, children need to acquire and maintain confidence in their ability to read and write. The biggest keys to effective reading and writing are practice and exposure to a broad range of language and its uses; this is how children gain understanding of what language can do. The schools will contribute to this understanding through the stories teachers read, the records and tapes children listen to, and the many intentional elaborations of words and word meanings teachers provide. But the home is also important. Try to read a broad range of literature to your child: rhymes, poems, fables, folktales, classic stories, and biographies. Sing songs together and play games. Such experiences will make a critical difference in your child's learning. In addition, call attention to things in newspapers and magazines, leave written messages around for your child, and make sure that your *own* literacy is evident. It is important for your child to see you reading and writing—and enjoying it.

You should try to do some reading with your child on a regular basis. As your child moves forward through the grades, his or her schedule will become more active and self-initiated. You will probably find that it is not as easy as it once was to engage in daily reading together. At a minimum, though, try to spend some time on Sunday afternoons or evenings to read from authors such as Charles Dickens, Robert Louis Stevenson, James Fenimore Cooper, Charlotte Brontë, Jack London, Langston Hughes, Bret Harte, Alex Haley, or Louisa May Alcott. Your child's interest in the stories you read will tell you a great deal about his or her development in listening and comprehension.

As you read a story to your child, occasionally ask, "What does that remind you of? What do you see in your mind?" Mental images are important to ongoing learning. (You and your child might even try sketching the images.)

Using the basic format of one of the stories you read, write a story together with your child. You write the first few lines or paragraph, have your child write the second few lines or paragraph, and so on. This could be a long-term project that gives you a look at your child's understanding of story sequence and word meanings; it also encourages the child to write creatively. Save these stories so you and your child can look at them together at a later time.

Begin making a journal of good times together—possibly the highlights of a trip, vacation, or family holiday. You and your child can each make entries. Read through what you have written from time to time.

Read newspaper headlines together and try to figure out what the story is about. You might also make a point of reading aloud to each other one newspaper story every day. This will help make the newspaper important to your child, as well as provide reading practice.

Get in the habit of clipping from the newspaper things you think your child might find interesting—human interest stories, cartoons, news related to the local environment. Such pieces are natural starting points for conversation.

Committing things to memory is a good exercise throughout the intermediate and middle school years. Each of you memorize a poem or story to tell to the other—one in the fall and one in the spring. The presentations can be family events.

Buy books for your child for special occasions. This gives you a chance to structure later conversations about the book, by asking, "How was the book? What was the mystery?" and the like.

As your child reads, find time to ask, "What is the book about? Who are the characters? What are they like? Where does the story take place?" Most children like to talk about what they are reading, as long as they do not perceive the questions to be either suspicious inquisitions or rote inquiries devoid of real interest.

Folktales and myths are often part of the fourth grade curriculum. See what your child knows about Robin Hood, Johnny Appleseed, Paul Bunyan, King Arthur, Brer Rabbit, Zeus, Apollo, or Prometheus. Read folktales and myths to each other.

The *Guinness Book of World Records* is very popular with children in the intermediate grades. They are particularly fascinated by extremes: the biggest, smallest, loudest, quietest, and so on. Take turns finding records that really surprise you.

Ask your child to teach you how to use periods, commas, semicolons, question marks, and exclamation points. Your child's ability to explain these will show you a great deal about how well he or she understands them.

Shopping provides many opportunities to use both language and math. For example, you might ask your child to check the fat and cholesterol levels on various product labels or find out the best buy for a particular item. The child can also be assigned to do part of the shopping on your list.

Play a word association game. You start by saying a word; your child is to say the first thing he or she thinks of. Then your child gives you a word, and so on.

Start doing crossword puzzles together. Children's sections of newspapers often have crosswords for children; many books of children's puzzles are also available.

Listen to music together. Talk about how it makes you feel—like "just sitting," "dreaming," "dancing," "marching." Move together to music. Also, share your views about various kinds of music. This will help your child enjoy music and also let you watch your child's music awareness grow.

See how many musical instruments each of you can name.

As a language-expanding conversation that will also tell you how much your child knows about many aspects of the world, say, "Let's tell each other all we know about Christopher Columbus." (Or George Washington Carver, hurricanes, whales, the Iroquois Indians, the moon, particular cities, outer space, electricity, engines, airplanes, different parts of the world, and so on.) You can see what words, people, and concepts are familiar to your child and also introduce new ones. This kind of activity is almost limitless. But you must listen carefully to your child's expressions. Do not be too hasty to correct or interrupt with information you think your child should know; that can come later, at the end of the activity or in a different conversation. It is important to let children express themselves fully instead of immediately quenching their pleasure with corrections.

Give your child increasingly complex models of airplanes, boats, houses, furniture, or cars to put together, following the instructions that are given. How effectively does your child follow the directions? Does he or she seem to grasp what to do? How do problems get solved? You might even draw and build something together.

Authorship is an important part of reading and writing. Keep asking your child about his or her favorite authors. Talk about new books together. Check out new titles through book reviews in the children's section of the newspaper or in the library. See how many books by your child's favorite authors are in the library. Many local libraries sponsor events where authors speak about their work or give readings from it; attend some of these with your child.

Keep using birthdays, holidays, and special family times as occasions for writing. Remind your child to write a letter to a grandmother, grandfather, or other close relative. Writing can be encouraged in lots of ways. For example, leave notes for your child, and ask him or her to leave notes for you. When you read what your child has written, pay attention to the ideas, the inventions, and the sustained stories. You will notice that your child's spelling and sentence structure are becoming more conventional in the fourth grade. Encourage your child to write stories and poems. Children in the intermediate and middle school years should also be encouraged to keep a journal, diary, or memory book; these activities not only give children writing practice but allow them to discover writing as a means of self-expression.

Invite your child to read one of his or her stories, poems, essays, or journal entries to you while it is in progress. This is a good time to gently let the child see whether the writing conveys what he or she wants it to. In addition, hearing your child's work at various stages both reinforces the point that revision is a natural part of writing and lets you watch your child's progress over time.

On a fairly regular basis, ask your child to bring home a favorite book from school to read to you. After your child has read the book, ask what he or she likes most about the story. As you listen to your child read the book, you will gain a good sense of your child's growth as a reader; you will also keep up with his or her changing interests.

Some words are spelled the same forward and backward. Take turns making up as many of these as you can: Mom, Dad, did, and so on.

Look at paintings together, either at museums or in books and magazines. Van Gogh, Gauguin, and Picasso have a great deal of appeal to children; you might also give some attention to abstract and geometric art. Ask your child what he or she likes in each painting. You will gain some insight into your child's growing understanding of color and into his or her imagination. Also ask about art activities in school. What is your child learning about painters, sculptors, and museum collections?

Ask often how your child likes various artworks—paintings, architecture, photographs, and music. This is your way of saying that you value artistic expression and of keeping your child's interest high. Take time to sing together. Ask your child to teach you a song he or she is learning in school.

Read plays aloud together, taking various parts. Your local library should have a children's theater or drama section. See how your child approaches reading a script.

Say, "Let's think of all the things rain does." It falls, splashes, drops, makes puddles, and so on. Continue the exercise with wind, a tornado, the sun, the moon, an animal, or any other noun that might suggest a variety of action words to your child.

Play games with antonyms (opposite words), such as good-bad, long-short, inside-outside, and loud-quiet; or synonyms (words with similar but slightly different meanings), such as evening-night, red-crimson, polite-courteous; or homonyms (words that are pronounced the same but have different meanings), such as sail-sale, tail-tale, two-too. For example, you could say, "I'll say a word and then you say the opposite." Or "Let's list all the words that sound the same." Suggest that your child write a letter to a public official or an organization about a cause that concerns him or her—to the Environmental Protection Agency, for example, about water quality in your state, or to the mayor of your city about a local issue. Both the conventions of this type of letter and the importance of speaking out on issues should have been part of your child's curriculum.

Early in their school careers children should be encouraged to assess their own progress as learners. In relation to reading and the language arts, ask your child such questions as, "How is your writing coming along?" "What causes you difficulty?" "What do you most enjoy writing?" Your child's responses to these questions will probably give you hints about games, activities, or pastimes to share with your child to boost his or her learning; they will also serve as a starting point for your own conversations with your child's teacher.

Mathematics

Like language, math is a subject in which it is important for children to build confidence. Fourth grade children continue to study quantities, size, scale, and estimation. Discussions of these qualities include continuing attention to mastering addition, subtraction, division, and multiplication. Rather than an exclusive focus on whole numbers, however, children work more with fractions, ratios, and percentages. They also do more problem solving with math.

The more concrete the learning, and the more children are encouraged to see mathematics in use all around them, the better. You can help by using math and the language of math around the house. Have your child help you with measuring tasks such as placing a picture on the wall, cutting out a pattern, building shelves, or papering a wall. Get your child to make estimates and judgments about distance and time, and play a lot of number-oriented games. Math is a natural area of learning that should always be interesting to children.

Engage in estimations with your child. Ask, "How far do you think it is from here to the corner? The mall? School?" "How tall do you think that tree is?" When you go shopping, say, "I can only spend $25, so you try to estimate when we are close to the limit." When traveling by car, see who can make the closest estimate of 1 mile, then 5 miles; use the odometer to check.

Make up story problems around math facts such as $12+12-6 \times \frac{1}{2}$. For example, 12 elephants were joined by 12 zebras, but 3 elephants and 3 zebras decided to go off on their own to take a nap. How many were then left? But because there wasn't enough grass to eat, half of them went to another part of the savanna. Now how many were left? It doesn't matter how silly the stories become.

Many games will reveal your child's knowledge of numbers as well as of words and directions. Play tic-tac-toe, dots, checkers, dominoes, concentration, hangman, Scrabble, and increasingly complex card games such as hearts, rummy, and cribbage. Keep playing games such as chess and Monopoly, which involve problem solving and mathematics.

Using a mileage chart as a prop, ask, "Is it farther from Seattle to Washington, D.C., or from New York to San Francisco?"

With a map of the United States, ask, "What is the shortest route from Boston to Grand Forks, North Dakota?" Or have your child trace routes to the homes of relatives and friends around the country—or the world.

While cooking or baking, ask your child to read recipes and measure the quantities of ingredients called for. This is a good way to see your child put math to use, and both of you will enjoy the companionship.

Fractions are an increasing part of the math curriculum in the fourth grade. Ask your child to explain, with examples, such fractions as 3/8, 5/12, 7/16. Make a graph of such measurements.

Ask your child to divide 60, 80, and 90 by 4, 5, and 6.

Work on number families together. For example, you could ask for combinations that relate to the numbers 4, 5, and 9: 4+5=9, 9-5=4, 9-4=5. Your child might ask you to do 5, 6, and 11: 5+6=11, 11-6=5, 11-5=6.

With a stopwatch, see how quickly your child can run 50 yards. Together, record and graph the times over several months. There is an almost limitless number of activities of this kind. You can also move into calculations such as, "How fast did you go per second in feet? In yards?" Or "If you continued to run at the same speed, how long would it take you to run 100 yards? Or 400 yards? How about 600 yards?" Such activities provide a useful link between mathematical computation and physical experience.

Make up problems. For example: "It takes us 3½ hours to get to Uncle Pat's house if we average 40 miles an hour. How long would it take if we went 50 miles an hour?"

The calculator should be very familiar to your child. Using a calculator, pick a number such as 29, then take turns adding a number from 1 to 5 into the memory. The objective is to see who can get to 29 first. This is a good mental math task and also another way to use the calculator.

The calculator can also be used in household tasks. Ask your child to help you with computational problems such as your checkbook, budget, floor covering measurements, and the like. Seeing math and the calculator as tools for dealing with everyday life is an important part of the curriculum.

Your fourth grade child is regularly using four- and five-digit numbers. Does he or she understand that 1,240 is 124 tens (or 12 hundreds and four 10s), that 16,280 is 162 hundreds and 8 tens or 16 thousands, 2 hundreds, and 8 tens? Ask your child to explain similar numbers that you encounter in the newspaper or on television.

Write numbers and identify the ones, tens, hundreds, thousands, ten thousands, and hundred thousands. For example, 963,550 = 9 hundred thousands, 6 ten thousands, 3 thousands, 5 hundreds, 5 tens, and 0 ones.

Play games with addition. Make up problems and ask each other for sums. For example: 9+3=___, 9+5=___, 24+10=___, and 37+9=___.

Ask your child to explain to you:
    How to add 2462 1390
      + 2712 + 2262
    How to subtract 2715 2262
      - 2462 - 1390

How to divide 30 by 3

96 by 2

Then ask your child, "Can you think of another way to do it?" Does your child know how to check these computations for accuracy?

Fourth graders should know the multiplication tables up through 12. Over the course of the year you and your child can work through such multiplication activities as 6x3=18, 6x4=24, 12x4=48, 12x6=72, and so on. Can your child devise story problems to go with these multiplication exercises? (For example, 12x6 might translate into "Twelve kids watched six videotapes each. How many videotapes did they watch all together?")

Ask your child to graph food prices—eggs, chicken, potatoes, and so on—each week for a month. Your child can check prices either at the store or in advertisements.

Pick a stock and follow its price in the newspapers—choose a company that your child will know something about, such as a fast food, soft drink, or video game manufacturer. Your child can make a bar graph showing the stock's performance and calculate how much he or she might have gained (or lost) with an investment.

Many graphs appear in newspapers and newsmagazines. Look at these with your child and ask him or her to explain them to you.

Do probability exercises together. Use a pair of dice to see if any numbers come up more often than the others. Ask if twelves are more or less likely than sixes, sevens, and eights? If so, why?

Estimate together the amount of water your family uses each week. Then ask your child to figure how how much there would be each month and each year and how much, on average, for each person in the household each week, month, and year; then estimate the total water use of your neighborhood. This exercise lets your child not only use his or her estimating, multiplying, and dividing skills but also encourages close examination of consumer habits.

Ask your child, "How well do you understand the math you are studying in school? What are you having difficulty with? Do you think you need help? What kind of help would be best?" Again, your child's responses may guide your interactions with both the child and his or her teacher.

Science and Health

Science study in the fourth grade remains concerned with the natural world—wind and rain, ponds, rivers, lakes, streams, the solar system, animals and plants, and food chains—though technology takes on added importance. Children observe nature and learn how things move through their various life cycles; they also observe various aspects of technology and learn about its development, uses, and problems. The intermediate grades are an important time for keeping curiosity alive and helping children expand their observation and problem-solving skills.

When you see a living creature on a walk, on television, or in a book or movie, classify it as an amphibian, mammal, bird, reptile, fish, insect, or crustacean. If you are not sure of a particular creature's category, research it together in a dictionary, encyclopedia, or animal book.

Observe the sky together. Ask, "Where will you find the sun in the early morning?" "At noon?" "In the evening?" And "What can we learn from the different kinds of clouds we see?"

Observe the moon together over several weeks; note whether you are looking at it at the same time every day or at different times. Note its location and draw its various shapes; be aware of the stars around it. Examine the moon chart in the weather section of your daily newspaper or on a calendar. There is almost no end to the astronomical observations you and your child can make. If, like many parents, you are not especially familiar with the sky, this exercise will be a good learning experience for you as well as for your child.

Graph the number of hours of daylight over a two-week period in the early fall, in January, and again in the late spring. Ask your child what is happening; how does he or she explain the differences in the length of the day?

Ask about the scientists your child is currently studying. Are men and women represented? What about people of color? What does your child know about these scientists and their work?

Take your child with you when you drop the car off to be serviced. Ask your child what the purpose of the car's oil and grease is.

Together you and your child can name various parts of the body: the heart, lungs, intestines, liver, arteries, white and red blood cells, and bones. Talk about their functions. Your fourth grader should have more sophisticated knowledge than he or she possessed earlier.

Engage in physical exercise together. This is a good invitation to ask your child what he or she is learning about staying healthy. During the intermediate years, as children approach puberty, it is important that they develop good attitudes about health.

Science in school increasingly gives attention to the sources of common things and to everyday processes. You and your child can investigate such questions as "Where does our water come from?" "What is added to make it safe for drinking?" "What is the source of our electricity?" "How is electricity stored?" "How does a motor work?" "What causes the cement to crack?" "How are bricks made?"

Your child is studying the role of technology in society. Ask about the effects of television on American families, about how computers have changed people's jobs, and how air travel has changed our understanding of people in other countries.

Ask, "How can we be sure our plants will grow?" Plan, plant, and tend a window box or garden plot with your child.

Go bird-watching (or bird counting) with a local nature group. You might also select a particular bird to study—learn how and where it builds its nest, what it eats, when and where it migrates, whether it is an endangered species, and so on.

Do simple science experiments with your child. For example, ask, "How could we determine which kind of paper towel would hold the most water?" or "How can we know what amount of water will be best for our growing plants?" Such experiments give a good indication of your child's thinking processes.

Ask your child about the science experiments he or she is doing in school. Have your child describe them: not just what was done, but what was learned.

See what your child knows about humidity and air.

Ask your child, "At what temperature does water freeze? Or boil?" Does your child know that there is more than one way of measuring temperature? On the Fahrenheit scale, water freezes at 32 degrees and boils at 212 degrees; on the centigrade scale, it freezes at 0 degrees and boils at 100 degrees.

Watch nature programs on television with your child. These programs offer opportunities for interesting conversations about everything from volcanic eruptions to the birds and plants of the Amazon rain forest. Your child's level of interest—and the questions he or she asks—are good indications of what the child is learning in school about nature.

Your child should be gaining mastery of three-dimensional forms. Can he or she child draw a sphere, a prism, a cylinder?

Ask your child to draw the solar system with as many planets as he or she can. If this is something you have done before and your child knows the planets and their names, ask what he or she has learned about each of the planets. This exercise will let you see what your child understands about the solar system. Try it at different times to see how the child's knowledge is growing.

Together with your child, make some graphs that compare current temperatures with those recorded the year before, or five years before, or with average and record high and low temperatures. Daily weather broadcasts and the weather section of the newspaper will give the average and record temperatures for each day; you and your child could consult old newspapers at the library for previous years' temperatures (or you may have recorded them together the previous year). Ask your child whether there has been a change over the years. This might be an occasion to talk about global warming and other possible reasons for shifts in temperature. What has your child learned about such things in school?

The life cycle is a large element of elementary school science; this is one of the reasons students keep mice and hamsters, hatch chicken eggs, and watch caterpillars turn into butterflies. It is also why many classrooms have made ties to senior centers and have invited mothers to bring their infants to class on occasion. See what your child has observed about baby mice, hamsters, chickens, or butterflies—or about human infants or older people. Your child's observations should be expanding with each passing year. If he or she has questions, suggest ways of finding out the answers.

Ask your child how to tell if trees, people, and dogs are young or old. What are their reasons?

In regard to nutrition, ask your child which foods are high in fat, protein, carbohydrates, cholesterol, and caffeine and what such measurements mean. Make a practice of reading nutrition labels together when you are shopping for or preparing food.

Visit a planetarium with your child. Try to go several times a year, as the programs generally change with the seasons. Before you go, discuss the program to see what your child already knows. After the show, talk about what each of you learned. Let your child see that you, as an adult, keep learning new things; this instills an appreciation of learning as a lifelong process.

The environment continues to be part of the curriculum in the fourth grade. Ask your child about things we can do to ensure a healthy environment. See what he or she knows about air, water, and noise pollution, toxic wastes, soil erosion, rain forest destruction, recycling, and landfills. Newspaper and magazine articles can serve as a starting point for conversations about these issues.

One important aspect of understanding newly learned material is being able to link it to other information, ideas, and concepts. Help your child practice making these connections. It often helps to "map" them out on a sheet of paper. For example, you might say, "Let's think of everything we can that relates to *sound*." Write SOUND in the center of a sheet of paper. Then write down all the images and ideas you can think of and connect them with lines.

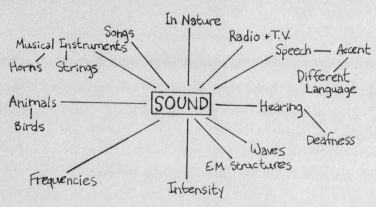

Try more exercises in making connections. You could start with ELECTRICITY. The related images and ideas might include currents, wires, lightning, batteries, nuclear energy, waterfalls, Benjamin Franklin, Thomas Edison, streetlights, plugs, light bulbs, sound, radio and television, and more. The larger the number of connections, the broader your child's understanding of the central concept.

Continue encouraging your child to examine his or her own learning. Ask, "How well do you understand the science you are learning in school? Is there anything you don't understand? What would you like to know more about?"

Social Studies

In the fourth grade, as in the earlier grades, the social studies continue to examine relationships within families and communities, while at the same time giving increasing attention to the geography and history of the state and the country. In many schools, fourth grade children also learn about other parts of the world. A child's work in social studies, as in the other subject areas, should be concrete and visible in the world. Many of the stories that are read to children, or that children read for themselves, have social studies themes.

Watch the television news together on occasion. Let the events on the news —human interest stories, hurricanes, elections, and the peoples and events of other countries—become a basis for conversation. You might also watch documentaries about historical figures with your child; biography is a good basis for helping children learn about history. Such documentaries are becoming more common, especially on public television and certain cable networks.

Children in the intermediate grades will notice and ask about the problems that they see around them: homelessness, drugs, conflict. It is good to talk about these issues. Ask your child whether he or she is discussing such topics in school. Does your child have unanswered questions?

Look at photographs together. Family pictures showing you and your child at different ages are a good choice. Ask, "What can you remember about these earlier times? What is different now?" You will find that your child will not tire of looking at pictures of family members.

Using a magazine such as *National Geographic* or photos from the newspaper or newsmagazines, see what your child knows about the relationships between *where* people live and *how* they live. For example, you might ask, "Why do you suppose people in certain parts of Queensland, Australia, build their houses on stilts?" (Because they live in a rain forest environment with lots of water and occasional floods.)

Ask what your child thinks it might have been like to live in different historical periods.

What countries does your child know about? Can your child find these countries on a globe or map? Discuss different countries together, perhaps reading about them in a magazine article or an encyclopedia.

Look at a bus or train schedule together. Does your child understand how it is organized? Can he or she make use of it?

Children celebrate a variety of holidays in school. Presidents' Day, Martin Luther King, Jr., Day, Veterans Day, Thanksgiving Day, and in some settings Cinco de Mayo receive the most attention. These celebrations are good opportunities to ask your child what he or she has learned about the presidents, Martin Luther King, Jr., and various national traditions; your child's awareness should be expanding each year.

Ask your child to share with you what he or she has learned about different ethnic and cultural groups in and around your community. What has your child learned about African Americans, Hispanics, Vietnamese, and Cambodians? Is your child reading books and stories by or about members of these groups?

Your child will be learning about the Native American peoples. See what Native American cultures your child has studied. Does he or she know about the Mayas? Ask how we know about the life of the American Indians before the Europeans came.

Ask your child to describe how a house is built, how wheat is harvested, how bread is made, how oil is carried from one part of the world to another, and so on. You will learn about your child's growing understanding of the world.

Share map activities. For example, you and your child can each draw a map of your neighborhood. Make up symbols to represent houses, stores, and so on. Put direction arrows in the map. For an extra challenge, try making the map accurate to scale—that is, keeping distances and sizes in their correct proportions.

Look at a map of your town or city with your child. Using the map, ask your child how to get to various landmarks. Move from local to state maps. Take turns finding particular cities and towns. Once you have found a town, ask your child how he or she would get there from home. How long might the trip take? Do either of you know something interesting about the town?

Using a globe or atlas, find the longitude and latitude of your town, the places where relatives live, and cities your child has heard about. Keep up the habit of asking your child, "What do you think?" about events and activities—politics, famine, protests, and such issues as animal rights. Listen carefully to your child's responses. This tells you a great deal about what your child understands. It also tells your child that his or her opinions mean something.

Children at school tend to be concerned with fairness and taking responsibility. Find out what is expected of your child in class—for example, keeping the room orderly, making sure books are put back onto shelves, picking up paper, taking care of equipment or animals, or working in cooperative groups in which children take turns fulfilling different responsibilities.

Your child is likely to be studying aspects of local and state history. With regard to a historical event, ask, "Why did that happen?" See whether your child can go beyond a recital of events to explain the underlying reasons for them.

Talk about the age of exploration with your child. Why did people from England, Spain, and France come to the Americas? Where did they establish settlements?

Problem solving is a vitally important skill. Get your child involved in the process of identifying problems and developing solutions. For example, you might ask, "What should we do? We need to decide what to plant in our garden" or "What shall we do this Saturday?" or "Which movie should we see?" Ask your child for suggestions and the reasons behind the suggestions. Share some of your own ideas. Together you can come up with a list of possible solutions.

A sense of history is important to ongoing learning. You might ask, "Do you know what our town (or city, or community) was like a hundred years ago? How did people travel then? How did they cook? How did they make a living? What was life like for children back then?" Expect your fourth grader to have a good deal of information about such matters.

Engage in community service activities together. Work at a food shelter, or contribute time to various charities. Many charitable organizations and medical research groups sponsor walks as fund raisers. Such activities are a chance to discuss the importance of service as part of citizenship.

Visit historical museums or sites together; such sites can be revisited at different points in the child's education. During these visits, talk about how people lived in other times. What are the differences between past and present ways of life? What are the similarities?

Take turns naming features of the physical landscape. For example, each of you in turn can name a land feature such as a cape, cliff, valley, peninsula, plain, mountain, or hill; you can do the same things with bodies of water (bay, sea, river, lake, stream, gulf, and so on).

Ask your child to teach you something he or she has learned in school.

Make a game of naming state capitals (use an atlas or map to check each other's answers, if necessary). Each of you in turn names a state, and the other tries to name the capital.

Ask your child how his or her school could be better. What about the neighborhood? The city or town? What ideas does your child have for bringing about the suggested improvements? These topics can be returned to many times through the years; they help reinforce a sense of citizenship.

Inquire about the government of your city and state. Who are the political leaders? What parties do they belong to? How are laws made and enforced?

The United States is a land of immigrants. Remind your child where your family's ancestors came from; find the homeland(s) on a map. Make a point of following newspaper accounts of your country or countries of origin; perhaps your child can start a scrapbook. Ask your child about the backgrounds of other students in his or her class. What is your child learning about recent immigrants from Mexico, the Caribbean, Southeast Asia, and Eastern Europe. Why does your child think so many people have come to this country, and are continuing to come?

Work together on a chart or "map" of connections. You might start with MARTIN LUTHER KING, JR. The related ideas could include civil rights, nonviolence, "I have a dream," national holiday, African Americans, justice, the U.S. Constitution, desegregation, assassination, hero, and so on.

Say, "Let's see how many U.S. presidents we can name." Many encyclopedias or almanacs have lists of the presidents to verify or round out your own lists. Does your child know something interesting about any of the presidents?

The news is full of struggles for freedom in various parts of the world. Inquire about your child's understanding of these events. Can he or she compare them with similar events in American history?

Ask, "If I wanted to know more about the Aztec Indians, what would I do?"

Take walks through local cemeteries. Look for the oldest stones. Note how long people lived during various time periods, and the fact that many children died young (sometimes many in a single year, if there was an epidemic). Note also that names give clues to national origins. You can find links with history—perhaps people who were born or died in historic years such as 1865 or 1918. You can take such walks every year, and you will probably notice something new each time.

Ask your child to tell you about the legends and myths he or she is learning in school. If there are legends associated with your own cultural backgrounds, share them with your child. Find books of legends in the library and read them together.

Ask about the earliest settlers of your state. Discuss the state's geography, regional differences, and intellectual history. See what your child knows about famous writers, artists, explorers, or scientists your state has produced.

Plan a visit to an industrial plant—a good chance to see American industry at work. You will see how well your child understands how things are made. (Send for USA Plant Visits, Order #003-012-0041-7, Superintendent of Documents, U.S. Government Printing Office, Washington, DC, 20402. The document costs $2.80. You might suggest that your child write the letter of request.)

Ask your child, "How well do you understand the social studies you are learning in school? Is there anything you don't understand? What would you like to know more about?"

6 *Parents and Schools*

As I said in the introduction to this book, parents are critically important to their children's education. By reading to your children daily during the preschool and primary school years, including them in family conversations, listening to them, providing them with varied experiences, and understanding that play and the exploration of diverse objects and environments are vital elements of learning, you can contribute greatly to your children's development and help them become successful learners. Young children need the active interest of their parents. They need to see that their parents care about them and their learning. Furthermore, children should know that their parents value language and are inquisitive about the world—that their parents, in fact, are also learners.

As the elementary years proceed, it is crucial for parents to continue reading to their children, sharing interesting stories from the newspapers and magazines as well as from the rich literature of mythology, biography, and travel. They should take walks with their children, making note of the environment and posing interesting questions along the way. Playing board games that demand problem solving, or watching television and discussing the programs afterward, are also ways to share in a child's learning while fostering a healthy relationship.

As children get older and move through middle school and secondary school, their interactions with their parents necessarily change. But parents' support remains important. Parents will find that taking an interest in what their children are reading and writing is an excellent starting point for conversations, no matter what age the children are. They will also discover that they can learn a great deal from their adolescent children, who may be reading literature or studying historical and scientific topics that the parents either never knew or have forgotten.

The parents' partnership with the school is also important. Maintaining this partnership may seem easier and more natural when children are in the primary grades, but parents should consider it a priority throughout *all* the grades. In the best situations, teachers actively seek connections with parents. They call on the phone, write personal letters, and hold informal discussions. And they make certain that conferences are scheduled for times when parents are able to attend. If teachers do not do these things, then parents should ask *why*.

Parents should expect their children's teachers to explain fully what the school year will be like, what topics will be studied, what problems are to be explored, what is to be read, what kinds of writing will be done, how the teachers will assess their students' progress, and how parents will be kept informed. If this information is not made available to parents, the parents should ask for it regularly.

To make the most of whatever information teachers provide, parents should try to spend some time—a couple of days each year at a minimum—in their child's classroom, especially during the elementary school years. This gives parents valuable direct insight into what their children's educational experiences are like. It also helps them understand the intentions of their children's teachers, which makes interactions between parents and teachers more constructive.

Many teachers actively encourage parents to be classroom partners. Parents may share some of their own experiences, read to children, take small groups of children on field trips, and the like. A few hours each week for such participation is very useful to both parents and their children.

How should parents approach their children's teachers and the schools? In most cases the teacher-parent exchange will be relatively easy. Teachers *want* connections with parents. They understand well the importance of parents as first and ongoing educators of their children. But they also know that parents have not always been sufficiently involved with their children or particularly responsive to teachers' efforts to interact with them. Both parents and teachers must strive for constructive, reciprocal exchanges.

Parents know their children. They know their interests and preferences, how they approach new situations, and how much they understand of the world. Parents need to share this knowledge with teachers in order to help the teachers be more effective. If your son or daughter is unhappy with school, feels unsuccessful or bored, seems not to be making progress as a learner, or is unable to take part in many of the conversations outlined in chapter 5, make an appointment with the child's teacher. *This is an important first step.*

Your meeting with the teacher should not be confrontational or angry. There is no need for defensiveness or anxiety. Share your concerns in as natural a manner as possible. If you have sensed that your child is unhappy about school, the teacher has probably sensed this also. If you have noticed that your child has lost interest in reading, seems uninquisitive about the natural world, or appears vague about mathematics and its uses, the teacher has probably observed these attitudes too. Now is the time for you and the teacher to come together on behalf of the child. Together, parents and teachers can figure out how to proceed. You might ask how you can be more helpful. Can the teacher suggest ways for you to enlarge your child's understanding of math, science, or language? Also inquire about what the teacher will do. Establish a schedule for meeting again to determine what progress is being made, and *keep* the schedule. If you create and maintain a seriousness of purpose where your child's education is concerned, you have taken a vital step toward improving the child's education.

As I said at the beginning, this book is intended to bring parents, children, and teachers together in a productive exchange centered on school learning. Most children, being the natural learners they are, will make academic progress in school—but their progress will be far greater if their parents are actively involved.

The schools generally meet students' needs reasonably well, if not always well enough. But they will also do far better if parents join with teachers in an active partnership. Chapter 1 of this book describes some of the qualities of a healthy school learning environment. An active partnership between parents and schools is necessary if such environments are to become the reality in all schools. Teachers should be supported in their desire for smaller classes in the early years, for a wide range of instructional materials, for strong arts programs. By providing such support, parents benefit their children and all children.

Books Parents Might Find Useful

Armstrong, Thomas. *Awakening Your Child's Natural Genius.* Los Angeles: J. P. Tarcher, 1987.

————. *In Their Own Way: Discovery and Encouraging Your Child's Personal Learning Style.* Los Angeles: J. P. Tarcher, 1987.

Bissex, Glenda. *Gnys at Wrk: A Child Learns to Write and Read.* Cambridge: Harvard University Press, 1980.

Burns, Marilyn. *The I Hate Mathematics! Book.* Boston: Little, Brown, 1975.

Caulkins, Lucy M. *Lessons from a Child.* Portsmouth, NH: Heinemann, 1986.

Children's Television Workshop Parents' Guide to Learning. *Kids Who Love to Learn.* New York: Prentice Hall, 1989.

Clay, Marie. *Writing Begins at Home.* Portsmouth, NH: Heinemann, 1987.

Gardner, Howard. *Frames of Mind: The Theory of Multiple Intelligence.* New York: Basic Books, 1983.

Goodlad, John I. *A Place Called School.* New York: McGraw-Hill, 1987.

Healy, Jane. *Your Child's Growing Mind: A Parent's Guide to Learning from Birth to Adolescence.* New York: Doubleday, 1987.

Kline, Peter. *The Everyday Genius: Restoring Children's Natural Joy of Learning.* Arlington, VA: Great Ocean, 1988.

Lappe, Frances Moore. *What To Do After You Turn Off the TV.* New York: Ballantine, 1985.

Maeroff, Gene. *The School-Smart Parent*. New York: Random House, 1989.

Papert, Seymour. *Mindstorms: Children, Computers, and Powerful Ideas*. New York: Basic Books, 1980.

Rosner, Jerome. *Helping Children Overcome Learning Difficulties*. New York: Walker, 1979.

Schimmels, Cliff. *How To Help Your Child Survive and Thrive in Public Schools*. New York: Revell, 1982.

Schon, Isabel. *Books in Spanish for Children and Young Adults*. Metuchen, NJ: Scarecrow Press, 1985.

Singer, Dorothy, et al. *Use TV to Your Child's Advantage: The Parent's Guide*. Washington, DC: Acropolis, 1990.

Stein, Sara. *The Science Book*. Boston: Little, Brown, 1975.

Taylor, Denny. *Family Literacy: Young Children Learning to Read and Write*. Portsmouth, NH: Heinemann, 1983.

Weitzman, David. *My Backyard History Book*. Boston: Little, Brown, 1975.

Wilms, Denise, and Ilene Cooper. *A Guide to Non-Sexist Children's Books*. Chicago: Academy, 1987.

Several Guides to Good Literature for Elementary School–Age Children

American Library Association. *Opening Doors for Pre-School Children and Their Parents*. Washington, DC: American Library Association, 1981.

Jett-Simpson, May, ed. *Adventuring with Books*. Urbana, IL: National Council of Teachers of English, 1989.

Lamme, Linda. *Growing Up Reading: Sharing with Your Child the Joys of Reading.* Washington, DC: Acropolis, 1985.

Lipson, Eden Ross. *The New York Times Parent's Guide to the Best Books for Children.* New York: Times Books, 1991.

Lorrick, Nancy. *A Parent's Guide to Children's Reading.* New York: Bantam, 1982.

Pollock, Barbara. *The Black Experience in Children's Books.* New York: New York Public Libraries, 1984.

Booklists

Each Spring, *Booklist*, the journal of the American Library Association, publishes a list of notable books for children, based on "literary quality, originality of text and illustrations, design, format, subject matter of interest to children, and likelihood of acceptance by children."

The Fall issue of *The Reading Teacher*, published by the International Reading Association, lists books children themselves select each year as "best books." (Available at no charge by sending a stamped, self-addressed #10 envelope to the Children's Book Council, 67 Irving Place, New York, NY 10003.)

The Spring issue of *Social Education*, published by the National Council of the Social Studies, lists books selected each year that "are written primarily for children . . . ; emphasize human relations; present an original theme." (Available at no charge by sending a stamped, self-addressed #10 envelope to the Children's Book Council, 67 Irving Place, New York, NY 10003.)

The Spring issue of *Science and Children*, the journal of the National Science Teachers Association, lists children's books selected annually for readability and science accuracy and interest. (Available at no charge by sending a stamped, self-addressed #10 envelope to the Children's Book Council, 67 Irving Place, New York, NY 10003).

VITO PERRONE is Director of Teacher Education and Chair of Teaching, Curriculum, and Learning Environments at Harvard University. He has previous experience as a public school teacher, a university professor of history, education, and peace studies (University of North Dakota), and as dean of the New School and the Center for Teaching and Learning (both at the University of North Dakota). Dr. Perrone has written extensively about such issues as educational equity, humanities curriculum, progressive education, and evaluation. His most recent books are: *A Letter to Teachers: Reflections on Schooling and the Art of Teaching*; *Enlarging Student Assessment in Schools*; *Working Papers: Reflections on Teachers, Schools, and Communities*; *Visions of Peace*; and *Johanna Knudsen Miller: A Pioneer Teacher*.